Not Your
AVERAGE GIRL
NEXT Door

DETRA D. RICHARDS

Scripture quotations marked NLT are taken from the Holy Bible, New Living Translation, Copyright © 1996, 2004, 2015 by Tyndale House Foundation. Used by permission of Tyndale House Publishers, Inc., Carol Stream, Illinois 60188.

Additional scripture references are used with permission from Zondervan via Biblegateway.com

ISBN 978-1-950861-71-2
PRINTED IN THE UNITED STATES OF AMERICA

Disclaimer: This book contains content of a sensitive nature. The author seeks to be transparent about the accounts of this journey in order to help others.

His Glory Creations Publishing, LLC
Wendell, North Carolina

DEDICATION

This book is dedicated to all survivors and victims of any form of trauma all over the world, whether it was child molestation, domestic violence, or rape. There is a blessing on the other side of your struggle. There is a purpose behind the pain. God will turn your mess into a message; he will turn your test into a testimony. It is time to heal and forgive so you can finally say, "I Survived!"

"For I know the plans I have for you," says the Lord. "They are plans for good and not for disaster, to give you a future and a hope" Jeremiah 29:11 (NLT).

TABLE OF CONTENTS

PREFACE

All Eyes on Her

When she enters a room, she enters with her head held high. She walks with confidence and grace. Her skin is flawless and glows like a ray of sunshine. When she smiles, her teeth light up as if she just left the dentist office from receiving a whitening treatment. This girl has it all together. When she opens her mouth to speak, she speaks with so much eloquence. She may not be a size 10, but her body will grab your attention, especially those muscular legs. This woman has got it all together.

This woman appears to be loved by everyone. They smile. They hug her, and some even give her a kiss. This woman's got it all together. Why do people think so highly of her? In my eyes, she is just like the average girl next door. When I look at her face, I can see the concealer marks that she uses to cover her blemishes. Her lipstick is cracked and fading from her lips, and her body is not all that. Why do people love her so much? She looks like she has it all together. But do they really know who she really is?

As I sit and watch her in the atmosphere of worship, she is observed to have it all together because her worship appears to be for real. As she is introduced to preach the unadulterated Word of God, her words will demand your attention because you want to know more about this woman. As she begins to speak of her life experiences and her testimony of how good and merciful God is, it still makes me wonder, *how did she get to where she is? Where did she come from? Most importantly, why do these people love this woman so much?*

From what I see, she seems to be like an average girl next door. The only thing special about her is she said, "Yes," to the call of God on her life. She does not appear to be any different than me. There must be more to her than what I can see. There must be a story behind her praise. Her testimony is strong, and it will make you shed a tear or two. I do not know about anyone else, but I want to know more about this woman. Is she really just an average girl next door?

INTRODUCTION

This book is over two years in the making. I have started, stopped, and repeated the same process more than I can count. Until this time, God said, "My child enough is enough. You have a story to tell, and it needs to be told so get with it." Even with hearing the voice of the Lord over these past few years, I still was a procrastinator. I put distractions, people, and other things in front of what God's plan was for me. Whether it was illness, money, work, or family, it did not matter. I put everything before God. Again, I would hear his voice say, "My child get with the program and finish what we started." So, guess what? I finished what we started years ago.

As I look back over my life and think things over, I can say, "Hallelujah and Thank you, Lord." Yes, I can say this now, but I was a long way from giving God thanks a few years back.

I used to have pity party moments, the "Why me moments?" I would ask myself, "Why am I going through this? Why am I going through that?" People would see me and think I had all my stuff together. If they only knew that I cried at night because of the mental loneliness. I cried in the morning because God was so cruel, and I felt He hated me so much, that He woke me up again. I would contemplate ending my life because the pain was so deep. But I continued to grow, and my life continued to move forward, regardless of how I felt. This world was not stopping because of my ongoing pity parties or me feeling sorry for myself.

My self-image or my low self-esteem would sometimes get the best of me. I would look in the mirror and say, "Nobody wanted me. I'm too fat, I'm too ugly, I stink." I would go on hunger strikes because I could not take looking at myself. I would go days without eating, or I would take an overdose of ex-lax because how I viewed myself was horrible. There were so many things going through my mind daily, and sadly I believed them. I believed everything I thought about myself. *Why would anybody want me? I am damaged goods. I do not know how to love anyone because I do not know how to love myself.* Yes, I went through life just as everyone else did. I had boyfriends, marriages, and children. I was a daughter, sister, aunt, wife, minister, and grandmother, but none of this made me feel any better about myself. I still felt that my family and the world would still be better off without me. Because I believed those things about myself, I felt I was a coward. I would think about ending my life. I would even write about it, but I could not actually do it. That made me feel even worse about myself. I never thought I would consider myself as being a coward. Then again, why not think that? I felt I was everything else I called myself.

One day, my life turned around, and I knew it was nothing I had done but surrender to God all the pain I was feeling inside. See, I knew my entire family was praying for me. The timbers were sent up for me, and all I needed to do was reach up and grab one. With the little life or little hope I had in me, I did just that. I reached up and pulled one of those deep-rooted prayers off the shelf, and God begin a work in me.

The journey of healing from life's trauma is a journey you cannot take lightly. Healing is not something that can happen overnight. It was not like a sore, and you put a band-aide on it until it is completely healed. Although I had used a life size band-aide for years to cover up my wounds, this time, it did not work. I was needing complete healing from the inside out, and I could not do it alone. With the foundation of God being introduced to me at a young age, I had to reach back and bring it forth to begin my healing. I do not believe I ever stopped believing in God and in his marvelous works. I believe it kept me going and pushing forward, but sometimes I would get weak. Yet, I would keep moving. However, this thing called life had me entangled in hurt and unforgiveness. I could not see the forest for the trees.

Forgiveness had to be mastered before the healing could begin, but I had to first forgive myself for the things that happened to me. I had to realize my innocence as a child was TAKEN from me. I did not freely give it away. I had to forgive myself from thinking it was my fault. Then, I had to learn to forgive the man who raped me repeatedly for years. I had to forgive my parents for not saving me, even though I did not know how to use my words and ask for help. I had to learn to forgive the man who beat me for years and left me for dead. I had to forgive myself for being so weak and attempting suicide. I realized I had a long way to go because I was not at the point in my life of being ready to forgive and move on to be who God ordained me to be before I was formed in my mother's womb.

When I talk about taking journeys, I want you to understand it was a painful journey. I had to relive all I had gone through repeatedly. Honestly, I was too ashamed to admit I allowed myself to endure such heartache and pain. I did not want anyone to see that side of me or even know I was such a weak-willed person to allow someone to control my entire being. I did not want anyone to know, and I did not want to admit it to myself. But self-admitting the things that had happened to me was an eye opener and that was through many years of on and off therapy and on and off medications. I faked my way through life. People loved me, but who they loved was not real.

As I sit and begin to reveal the real me and how the many masks I wore over the years began to peel away, I want you to understand the face, the self-image that was developed behind the years of pain, and how unforgiveness can keep you from being whole. It can keep you from being the person God wants you to be. God said, "It is time, my Queen. It is time, my King, to untie the mask and finally let it go and be great." God made you in His image, and He did not wear a mask, so remove yours and live.

I want those who took the time to purchase and read this book to see themselves within the pages. I want you to see that you are more than just existing. You are here for a purpose, and it's time for you to find it. Find your will to forgive those who hurt you and forgive yourself for hurting others. Make things right with them and God. Ask God to cleanse you from the inside out, become that new creature according to 2 Corinthians 5:17, "Therefore, if any man *be* in Christ, *he is* a new creature: old things are passed away; behold, all things are become new." This could be you today. Accept it and begin to walk in victory. Begin to walk in your destiny. Remove the mask and finally see the real you. It might surprise you to know you are fearfully and wonderfully made in the image of God. Learn to love the true you, flaws and all.

CHAPTER ONE

THE BEGINNING OF THE BEGINNING

The old saying is that you do not get a chance to pick your family. Well, that is such a true statement, but looking back over my life, I wonder if I could have chosen my family. Who would they be? What would they look like? As you begin to read my life's journey, do not think it was all bad. I had a surprisingly good childhood, of course with challenges.

My life began on May 24, 1966, in Longview, Texas. I lived in a small area of town called Fox Hill. My mother was the youngest of twelve kids, and she was only sixteen years old when I was born. You would think that being born to a sixteen-year-old girl would be hard, but my mother had a huge loving family who stepped up to the plate. As for who my mother says my father is/was a mystery to me. She said my biological father died before I was born due to complication of leukemia. However, there was always a rumor on the hill that my father was an older man name Lucious Marshall (everyone knew him by the name of Jr. Marshall). I still tease my mother to this day about who my father is.

When I was only six months old, my mother met and married a man by the name of Morris Williams, aka Cat Daddy, or Pork Chop. He later moved us along with his mother to Dallas, Texas, where our new life began. Later, there were two more children born from this marriage. Like with most children, my life started with me being a happy well-rounded little girl; most people will tell you that I was a tomboy. I would run and jump around with the best of them. I would climb trees, play football, and out-run any man, boy, or child in the neighborhood. There was nothing a boy could do that I could not do better. I was one of those girls.

My dad had a great job, and he provided very well for the family financially. He did not waste money. As children, we did not get much of what we wanted, but all our needs were met. If you looked at my family from the outside, you would think we were the model family. We lived in a middle-class neighborhood; our family was the fourth black family but the second black family with children. There was not a lot to do because most of the white children were not allowed to play with us, but we still had fun with the kids we could play with. As children, we did not understand this was racism, and honestly it did not matter to us. We found ways to play with some of the white children. We had a mom and dad in the home who both worked. My grandmother also lived with us. She worked part-time cleaning houses but was always there when we got home from school. As the sun began to set, all the homework was done, the dinner dishes were washed, and we were settling in for the night. When Dad arrived home, we walked on eggshells. We never knew what type of mood he would be in. My father was an alcoholic and an abuser. He would beat my mom with broom handles, the butt of a gun, his fists, or whatever else he could find. Although he would send us outside or to our rooms, we could still hear what was going on, and we could see the results of the beating when we saw our mother the next day. My mother was not perfect, and she did some things she should not have, but nothing she did deserved the beatings she received. She drank a little too much, and that would sometimes make the beatings worse because she would talk back. That only made him angrier and the beatings got worse. We could hear our grandmother say, "Morris, Jr! Leave that woman alone." He never would until he was finished. That was the physical, mental, and emotional pain she went through just to keep the family together.

Believe it or not, we were Christians. We attended church on Wednesday nights, Saturdays for choir rehearsals, and other auxiliary meetings and right back at it early Sunday mornings. At first, my mother would not attend church with us because she would sometimes be working or just did not want to go, but Grandma Jessie would make sure we were there. At the age of nine, I was baptized mainly because I was seeing everybody else do it, so I wanted to go and play in the water. Truly not understanding what being baptized meant, I was happy just to do what everyone else was doing. To be honest, I had a dark secret that I was hoping being baptized would wash it away, not knowing that dark secret would only get worse as I got older.

CHAPTER TWO

FROM DARKNESS TO THE DIM LIGHT

This is where the story gets real, and I must caution you, I will be very transparent because the truth must be told. Although worst things happen in the dark, remember it can also be sunny outside, and you can still be in darkness.

Around 1974, weeks after my eighth birthday, I was sleeping in my bedroom that I shared with my baby sister, who was three years younger than me. We did not have a TV in our room nor a night light, which means we slept in pure darkness. That night my life began to change. I don't remember the exact time, but it was dark. Suddenly, I felt a light touch shaking my big toe. I woke up, and all I could see was an extremely dark figure standing at the end of my bed waving for me to follow him. There was light from the moon glowing through the blinds. I got up and followed him because I was innocent and had no clue what this was all about. To be honest, I really did not know who had come in to wake me. The only persons I could think of were my uncle or dad. These were the only men in the house. I thought my dad was waking me up because we forgot to wash the dishes, which was a chore for all the kids to do each night.

Regardless of who, I followed him into the garage. At that time, I finally realized who it was but still not understanding what was going on. He made me lay down on a towel, but I could still feel the cold concrete floor. There was a door in the living room that led directly into the garage, so we did not have to go outside to enter it. As I lay there on the cold concrete floor, he raised up my pajama top and began rubbing my chest, which was flat. He would suck on my nipples, which hurt. While doing this to me, he would be holding his penis in his hand, rubbing his hand up and down, and moaning. I would still just be laying there in a daze. When he would finally ejaculate, he would pull my shirt down and tell me to go my room. I would get up off the cold concrete floor shaking, crying, and wondering what just happened. I was not naive to sex. I knew what a penis and a vagina were. I had older cousins. When we would go to the country to visit family, me and my younger cousins would watch the older kids from the hill, through a window, have sex. So, that was not a surprise to me, but what was happening to me was a surprise.

That dark figure would enter my room sometimes every night. Then, over time it became normal. When it would not happen, I would think I had done something wrong. I kind of knew what he was doing was wrong because I was a child, and he was a grown man, but I began to like the attention I was getting. Just as if I was a grown woman, he touched areas of my body that made me feel good. This went on for years before he began to rub my vagina, inside and out. He would wake me up, take me to the garage, lay me down, pull my gown up or my pajama bottom down and begin to rub my clitoris. To be honest, it began to feel good. One time, he was rubbing my clitoris with his finger, and I began to quiver. He moaned, ejaculated, and was done.

This was confusing to me because I had no idea what had just happened because it had never happened before. So, I went through my days thinking about that night and what it felt like. It felt good, but why did it feel so good. I just did not understand. I guess I may have been around nine or ten years old. I began to want to feel that sensation again, so I learned how to play with my clitoris myself to just feel that sensation again. Over time, this became a habit for me. I would masturbate morning, noon, and night. Sometimes I could not go to the bathroom without wanting to get that sensation feeling again.

Here comes the shift. I had to think long and hard about the timing of everything. I had written in the past that my period started before the sexual abuse, but as I reflect now, the actual penetration of the sexual abuse was before my menstrual period. Most people remember their first sexual encounter as something good and memorable. Well, my first time was not good or memorable. It was memorable, which means a memory I would never forget. Well, I guess you can say that I graduated from the fondling and sucking of the nipples to the next stage. I really cannot remember the exact time of year. I just know that night changed my life forever. I was always afraid of the unknown about what was going to happen next.

Well, this one time, the unknown became known to me. His normal routine did not change; it would be late and dark. Everyone would be in their rooms asleep with their doors closed, and my dear old uncle would come in the room, stand at the foot of my bed, and wake me. As always, I got up, and followed him into the garage. This time, it was different. This was the first time he laid down a thick blanket. I thought it was odd. He would always lay down a towel. I got so use to him doing things to my body that I would go ahead and raise up my pajama top so he could rub and suck my nipples, and I pulled down my pajama bottoms just a little so he could touch my vagina. Again, this time was different. He told me to take my pajama bottoms off. So, I did. To be honest, all these years of him abusing me, I had never seen his penis. This time, he pulled down his pants and underwear, and I saw his penis. I was shocked because it was something I had never seen in person, on pictures of course, but never in person. He laid me down and opened my legs. He began to rub my vagina inside with his hand. Then, he would rub on the outside. Man, this time it hurt, and I guess he could tell because he told me not to move or say anything. Now, I thought his finger hurt, but when he attempted to insert his penis in my vagina, that is when the real pain began. He kept trying and trying to get it in, but it just would not go, and he was breathing heavy and hard. Then, he began to get mad and complained about my vagina being dry. He tried to moisten my vagina by inserting his finger again, but still, there was no moisture. His head went between my legs, and I had no clue what he was doing. Suddenly, I felt an instant moisture as he took his saliva and spat on my vagina to get it wet, rubbing his spit into the hole of my vagina. He then got back into position to insert his penis in me, and it was the worse feeling in the world. It hurt so bad all I could do was cry and tense up my body, not realizing that made it worse. This was the first time he was so rough. Each motion, I hated. it hurts so bad, and as the tears rolled down my face, I just knew he was going to stop, but he did not. He was breathing and moaning, but I was crying. When he finished, he said, "You are now a woman, and things are going to be good between us." I did not know exactly what that meant. It just put more fear in me. As I was getting up, I finally asked, "Why are you doing this to me?" The next words out of his mouth hurt me as much as him penetrating me. He said, "If you were my REAL niece, I would not be doing this to you. Since you are not really related to me, it is okay." I knew my father wasn't my blood father, but he was still my father, and I had always thought I was family. I had never felt that I did not belong, even though my last name was different. No one had ever treated me like I did not belong until that very moment. From that day forward, I felt I did not belong in my family. Days would go by, and I would still remember what he said. It would hurt all over again. Weeks and days had passed, and I would wonder if anyone could tell that I was no longer a little girl, but no one seemed to notice anything different about me.

It was a hot summer day, and my brother and sister were outside. I had run inside to use the bathroom. While in the bathroom, as I wiped, I noticed I was still wet, and I wiped again. Then, I looked down and there was blood. I begin to scream because in my household no one discussed anything about your body or what, as a girl, was going to happen to you once you became older. I screamed as if someone had hit me over the head with something. My mother and grandmother ran to the bathroom to see what was wrong. Then, they started laughing. I was amazed and could not understand what they were laughing at. It was really making me mad because I was crying, and they were laughing. My mother said, "Girl, stop that crying. You just got your period." I had heard what a period was from some of the older girls at school. Because I was only nine, I did not think it would happen to me. After I learned what it was, I felt so dirty and nasty, but the good thing that came out of it was my uncle would not wake me up at night. Therefore, I wished for my period to stay on forever. Well, of course with me starting my period, it did not stop the sexual abuse from happening. It really made things worse.

The horror of my sexual abuse went on for years, and I felt as if I did not belong to anyone. For years, I felt like an outsider but still went on each day as if nothing was wrong. See, I learned at an incredibly young age that what happens in this house, stays in the house. So, I would not dare tell anyone what was going on. At times, after he would have sex with me, he would tell me, "If you tell anyone, I will kill your Mommy." He would even say he would kill my siblings. With him saying that to me, I knew I could not tell anyone. I was a young girl who lived in fear daily, not knowing the next time my dad would beat my mom or if I would let something slip out about my uncle raping me, and he would kill me and my whole family. I just did not know what to do, so I buried my feelings and never told anyone. As time went on, I would wonder to myself even more, *can they see something is different about me? Can they see by the way I walk or the way I talk that I am no longer that innocent little girl?* No, no one paid attention. No one could see the pain I was hiding. How could they not see that I was different? As I got older, I wondered, *how could they see when I have no voice of my own?* So, life went on. Some may consider that normal, whatever that was.

Not only did my life change a few years back, it was only getting worse. At the tender age of twelve, I began to feel sick in the morning, and I could not hold down food. I went from an active teenager that loved playing sports and hanging outside with all the other kids in the neighborhood to a teenager who only wanted to sleep and eat. My mother decided to take me to the doctor. At the doctor's office, I overheard my mother say, "Who would do this to my baby? How could my twelve-year-old daughter be pregnant?" But she did not ask me. No one asked me, not even the doctor. The doctor talked to my mom about options. Everyone just assumed I'd had sex and got pregnant. When we got home, I could hear my mom and dad arguing about me and what they were going to do about the situation. Both were saying, "We cannot tell anyone." Again, no one asked me. It was as if I did not exist, but I knew I did because that horrible ordeal was happening to me. A few days later, my mom had taken me to another doctor's appointment at a different office. There was a weird smell, and people just looked at me. I knew how to read, so I was seeing posters with the word abortion on them and other things showing the different diagrams of babies at different stages of development. I had no clue how far along I was, but I could only guess I was not that far along because I was there at the clinic. We went to the back, and about thirty minutes later the procedure was over. I cramped and bled so badly. All I could do was lay down in the backseat of the car.

Again, I still wondered, "Why is my mother not talking to me about what had just happened to me?" When we arrived home, there was a male detective sitting in our living room. He introduced himself to me and asked my mother if he could talk to me in private. She said, "Yes." I had no clue how the police found out. I was terrified because I thought I was going to jail. I thought he knew I'd just killed a baby. He was a nice man, and we talked about sports and foods I liked. Then, it happened. He asked the question I was sure my parents should have asked. The detective came straight out and asked me if I knew what sex was, and I explained to him what I thought it was. He told me I was right. He then asked me who I had been having sex with. I looked him straight in the eyes and said, "A dark figure. His name is W." I begged him to not tell my parents. He smiled and spoke to my parents in private. When the detective left, my mom and my grandmother were both crying. I knew they were going to finally ask the question, but they never did.

A few months later, my grandmother and my uncle had left the house to go and meet with his attorney. See, my uncle had a long criminal record, and he had been in and out of jail ever since I'd known him. When they arrived back home, my grandmother looked at me with tears in her eyes and asked, "Why did you not tell me?" I could not say a word. I just stared at her. About a week or two later, my uncle was arrested and criminally charged with five counts of indecent liberties with a child under the age of fifteen. I thought it was all about me, but to tell the truth, he was also charged with molesting another girl in the neighborhood. The police were already investigating, so when they heard I was pregnant, and he lived in the house with us, that moved the investigation to our home. Now, I did not know the ends and outs of it all. I only knew he was finally gone. No one, absolutely no one, in my family ever said anything about it to me. Mostly, I remember my grandmother walking around the house crying when they took my uncle to jail. He got twenty-five years to life for the various crimes and for being a repeat offender.

After he was gone, I felt safe again. I was turning into that active little girl again, yet something just was not right with me. I could feel it. I was still hiding in the bathroom or in my room masturbating just to get that sensation. You would think because the sexual abuse was over that I would be okay and back to normal. I did not know what normal was. How do you go back to life as usual after experiencing the things I had gone through? I had gone without sex for a while, and my body was beginning to react in a way it shouldn't have been reacting. I was already masturbating, but that was beginning to not be enough. I was ready to feel the real thing inside of me. So, I became very promiscuous, and let me tell you, it was not hard to find boys who were willing and able to take care of those feelings I was having. I began to have a little reputation, but I did not care. All I wanted to do was have sex to get that feeling. There were times that I would feel bad after having sex with random boys. Then, there were times when I just didn't care.

Things did not get better in high school. I had a cute, fine boyfriend, and we dated throughout my whole high school years. We were very sexually active; we would do it at a drop of a hat. We would have sex under the staircase, in the bathroom, in the locker room, on the school bus, and behind the building. Honestly, it was wherever we could get a few minutes alone. He was my breakfast, lunch, and dinner. Some nights, I would sneak out of the bedroom window and meet him down the street at the park. We would have sex in the car or in the woods. I did not realize that I was now experiencing teen physical abuse. He would hit me, kick me, and throw water or whatever he was drinking in my face for no reason, and I would trail behind him like a puppy dog. He and his boys would laugh at me, but that would not stop me. I would still be there for him to use and abuse. He would have sex with other girls. He would touch and rub their butts in front of me, and I would cry but still be there for whenever he needed me. I had no clue at that time what I was going through. I only knew he said he loved me. I felt love because I was his girlfriend, and we had a lot of sex. Man, I had a lot to learn about life. But I was damaged and did not know it. My home life was screwed up, and my teenage life was too. My parents were already divorced, and I was happy about that because my mom was not getting beat any longer. Life was rather good by that point. I was busy in sports, and my senior year was approaching. My high school sweetheart was still who he was, and he was not about to change. So, I took things for what they were. The best thing about my senior year was that I was working and only going to school half the day. I was making and spending my own money. I graduated high school on May 22, 1984, and again life was good. My boyfriend went into the Army, and of course I was lost and did a lot of crazy things. Shortly after he was discharged, he started dating another girl and got her pregnant. That was the end of us. I was heartbroken, but believe it or not, my life was moving forward, and I was happy.

CHAPTER THREE

FROM THE MARVELOUS LIGHT
BACK TO DARKNESS

I am sure chapter two was a little too transparent and detailed for some, but if you really want to know the person I am, well you have to know the good, the bad, and the ugly.

I have had some good days, and I have had some bad days, but I won't complain. I am in no way saying that my life has always been bad and full of pain. There were some good days when I could just put everything I had gone through and everything I was currently going through behind me. I could smile and be happy with the best of them. Then, there were times when I felt that life was not worth living. After the sexual abuse and the high school teen physical abuse, I still had not learned how to just be me. Hell, I did not even know who I was as a person. Over the next year, things did get a little better.

At this time, I was working and making my own money, I was more interested in shopping and buying stuff for my siblings. This was the first time I felt I had control over my life. I could go to work if I wanted, and it was my decision. See, as a child, my body was not mine. As a teenager, my body was not mine either. However, as an upcoming adult, I finally found something that was mine. That was the little money I was earning. I was eighteen, almost nineteen, and my dad was getting on my nerves. He talked about saving money, possibly going to college, and I was not hearing none of that. So, one Friday night, I had gone to church with a friend, and he introduced me to a friend of his. This man was so cute. He was light-skinned and had a beautiful smile. What topped it all off, he was a preacher. I do not know what it is about preachers. Women just fell head over heels in love with them, and I was no different. We dated a few months, and by this time, I felt that he loved me. We had not had sex because he said he did not believe in sex before marriage. He then popped the question and asked me to marry him. Not even thinking twice about it, I said yes. I was married at the age of nineteen, and he was twenty-eight years old. His age did not matter because he loved me, and I loved him. That was the first time somebody wanted me and not just for sex. We lived a good life for a while. He was a hard worker and a great provider. On the Sundays when he would preach, I would sing his favorite hymn, and I wasn't what you would call a great singer, but just to know that is what he asked me to do, and God was pleased with our ministry. I could not pass up the opportunity to stand next to my wonderful husband and sing for the Lord. "Because He Lives" was his favorite song for me to sing. The words to that song could bring a sinner running down the aisles, asking what I must do to be saved. I never noticed that each Sunday he preached there were a vast number of women joining the church we attended. I was so naive and blind I could not see what was going on right in front of my eyes. We were married just a short time, and I got pregnant. Lord, I was scared. You see, I never wanted children. I did not feel I had the motherly instinct to raise and care for a child, but

God saw different. I gave birth to a beautiful baby boy. He has brought much joy into my life, still to this day.

Well, shortly after he was born, the truth began to reveal itself. The women's ministry of the church would come to the house with prepared food. They would sit and talk with me during the day or call to see how I was doing. A few months went by, and he would come home from work and spend time with us. When Friday rolled around, he would pack a bag, make sure we had food, and he would be gone until Sunday morning just before it was time to get ready for church. I never questioned what he did, but I was not stupid. I knew what was going on, but he was my husband, my pastor, and the father of my son. What was I to do? Where were we to go? I was only working part-time as a night auditor at a hotel. I did not make much money, but I used what I made to make things work because over time he stopped bringing his money home. He would come home on Sunday morning with hickeys all over his chest, but did I question? I did not. I went on as if everything was okay. We went to church as a family, and I smiled as if I had the whole world at my feet. Things began to slowly change because I started to notice a lady at the church being way too friendly with my husband. Later, I discovered that she was only one of the many women who had been having a long-time affair with my husband. Suddenly, I began to feel that everyone was watching and talking about me. I became extremely uncomfortable attending church, so, there were times I would miss a Sunday here and there, but I would always go back. One Friday night was the last straw. As he was preparing to leave for the weekend, he was ironing his shirt on the living room floor (because we did not have an ironing board). Our son was just learning to crawl, and his father left the iron plugged up on the floor. My precious child crawled right into the iron and burned the side of his face. My baby screamed, but do you think that stopped his father from leaving? Nope, it did not. He still left without even caring how I was going to stop our child from crying or even how I was going to take care of him while he was out on whatever mission he was on. Well, a gentleman who lived two doors down heard my precious son screaming and came to check on us. I explained to him what happened. He worked as a mechanic, so he was always getting burned. He gave me some cream for my baby's face and told me what to do. So, over a few hours, my baby began to feel better.

Let's fast forward a few weeks. It was Friday night again, and my husband was packing his bag to leave. Once he left, I called my father and told him I could not take it anymore. I needed to get out of there. The next day my father and a few of his friends came to our apartment and moved me and my son out. We lived with my dad until I could get myself back together. My husband never came looking for us. He called but that was it. A year later we were divorced, and there I was twenty-two years old with a two-year-old son, and I was living in the home where I was sexually abused, the home where I witnessed my mother being beaten so many times. I was back at the beginning, but it was not the same. We all were much older. The garage was no longer a garage. It was a den. However, I still viewed it as a garage.

At this time, I began working as a receptionist and financial aid assistant at one of the local business colleges. I was still living with my father, and each day I rode public transportation to work. The job was not hard, and I really enjoyed what I did. I did not feel like I had to impress anyone. I could honestly be myself. I would greet the students as they entered the door. I could smile and have fun with the best of them, but to be honest I was lonely and sad. Then, one day I met a young man. His smile lit up my dark, dull life. He would come to my desk every morning and give me a Dr. Pepper and ask how I was doing. One thing that attracted me to him is he paid attention to me. He knew I liked Dr. Pepper. He knew I rode the city bus to work, and he gave me a monthly bus pass. This went on for a while. Then, all of a sudden, I found myself kind of liking him. This man treated me like no other. He would buy me things, walk me to the bus stop, and sometimes rode the bus with me. It did not take much to make me happy or to impress me. I was simple, and he saw that in me. All I really wanted was for someone to spend personal time with me, love me, touch me, and be good to me. He started out that way. He was great to my son and to me. We eventually moved in together, and I then learned that he could cook, clean, and the sex was the best I'd ever had. He would make sure every inch of my body was touched, and he took pleasure in knowing that I was completely satisfied sexually. All I knew was missionary sex. I did not know any of the other things that went along with being sexually pleased. I had never had anal or oral sex and was in awe when it was introduced to me. To be honest, I was rather embarrassed to think that people were doing such things. Over time, he assured me that there was nothing wrong with what we were doing.

Well, all of this was good while it lasted. A few months later, things began to change in our life. People always wonder how the abuse starts. When did you notice the red flags? As I look back now, the red flags were there all along. I just thought he loved me and wanted to protect me by knowing my every move. I did not realize with me telling him where I was going, who I was with, and how long I was going to be gone was a clear sign of him being controlling. Even when I was out with my mom and sister, I still had to come home and report our every move. Shortly, we would be wrestling or play fighting, and he would hit me hard or twist my arm. I would say it hurt. He would apologize, and things would be okay. Then, he started belittling me, telling me everything I did wrong, talking about how fat I was getting, and how ugly I was. He would say things like, "Don't nobody want you but me." I had revealed to him things that I had gone through in my life as a child, and that was an open invitation for him to start the emotional and mental abuse process. Never did I know that the patten of abuse was beginning. I would be feeling so bad about myself that I really did not care what I looked like. I would not even look people in their eyes. I would hold my head down, mainly because if I looked at someone, especially a man, he thought I was flirting with him. He would accuse me and say awful things. He would call me a bitch, a whore, and a liar. The first time he hit me, should have been the last time. I was naive and thought he was smoking cigarettes but later found out that he was smoking marijuana and crack. I confronted him one day, and he slapped me so hard that I got dizzy, but I still stayed because he said he loved me, and he would never do it again. For a while, things were good, and we got married. I later got pregnant but had a miscarriage, mainly because the physical abuse had begun again. He would get mad and punch me in the stomach or sometimes even kick me, and I would bleed out and lose yet another baby. I had two miscarriages before God blessed us with a healthy baby boy who added to the joy my oldest son had already given me. Things were good for a while. However, I could not hold down a full-time job because of the abuse, so I worked various temporary jobs. This man was a great father to the children, but he was an awful husband to me. He went from slapping me to kicking, hitting, punching, and finally raping me numerous times. One time, after he raped me, I said, "Here I go again. My body is no longer my body." One time, he held me down with a knife to my throat, telling me if I did not give him oral sex until he ejaculated, he would kill me. I did not know the effects that drugs had on someone's system, especially their mental state of mind. He was hallucinating, thinking someone else was in the house, or someone had just gone out the door, or window. One time, he fractured my nose because he came home from hanging out and the maintenance man was leaving out as he was walking in. He swore I had just had sex with him, so, he had to put on his doctor's eyes and checked my vagina. No matter what I said, it did not matter. His way of thinking was the right way. He checked my vagina by putting his fingers inside of me, and with that form of sexually act whether in a good way or bad way, a normal response a woman would become sexually arouse. I became wet, and he just assumed I had sex with someone else, so he would rape me then he would start beating me, and he hit me so hard in my face that he fractured my nose. Each time I got an injury, he would not let me go to the doctor, so my nose evidently healed, but on the bridge of my nose, there is a knot where it did not heal properly. He would beat me and then want to have sex, and of course I did not want to. After a while, I would just have sex with him because if I did not, he would take it. The pain was so bad. He would want vaginal and anal sex, which was the worse, but I had no choice because again my body was not my body. To go back a little further, right before going into the hospital to have our son, we had sex before leaving the house. When we got to the hospital, we went into the bathroom to have sex again. He was the type of man that had to have sex everyday regardless of if I was on my period or not.

During the physical abuse and still going out into the community, it was not hard to hide or make up a lie about the bruises. Whatever I told people, they would believe it. One time, I had a black eye. I told people I reached up into the cabinet and a can fell out. People believed me, so I kept lying, and it got easier for me to do. I was isolated from my family and friends, so they did not see the bruises because I could not go anywhere. Do not think that I just took the abuse and never did anything about it or try to leave. I did. At times, I would call the police or either a neighbor would call the police because the beating was so bad, and he would go to jail for a few days, or they would take me to a shelter. That was short lived because I felt I needed to be home, so I went back, and things were good for a while. Another time, he attempted to brand his initials on the inside of my thighs with a wire coat hanger that he put on the stove to get hot (but I fought him this time and WON). One evening, the kids were with my sister, and we were in the house just hanging out watching TV or something. He called me into the bathroom, and he had some supplies on the countertop: chore boy, a little piece of a broken antenna, a spoon, and his lighter. I had no clue what any of this was being used for. He pulled out a piece of foil that had some clear peddle in it. Again, I had no clue what he was doing. He asked me to smoke some with him. I said, "Somewhat?" He said, Crack." I told him that I would never do that. I had never had a drink nor anything to smoke, especially illegal drugs. Oh, I spoke up quickly and said, "There is no way I'm going to let that stuff in my system." He continued to try to talk me into it, but shortly he tried to force me to do it, and I turned him down again. He got angry and grabbed my right arm and twisted it so hard until I heard a pop. This time, I did go to the doctor, and it was fractured. The doctor asked me what happened. As always, I lied and said we were wrestling, and we got a little rough. What was I supposed to say? My husband was standing right there. There were times he would smoke crack and could not get an erection. He blamed me for it, and he would beat me. I would get punched in the mouth when I talked back.

My life was a roller coaster. There were so many ups and downs that I did not know which one I was supposed to enjoy. Over time, I started to feel trapped. I felt the only way out was to kill myself. My first attempted suicide was Labor Day weekend in 1992 or 1993. I cannot remember the exact year. My mom had taken the kids out of town with her, so we were home alone. My husband and I had hung out with his sister that whole day and we did what they liked, drugs and drinking. I did neither but still had to sit there. We were headed home, and he wanted more drugs but did not have any more money. Of course, I did not have any either, so he wanted to pawn my wedding ring. We had nothing else to pawn because he had already pawned everything we had of value. I, of course, told him no, and he hit me so hard across the face that my glasses fell off, and my lip started bleeding. Well, of course from there, we pawned my wedding rings, and he got enough money to go get him another round of whatever it was he was smoking. On the drive home, I made it up in my mind that was it. I was not going to go through that anymore. I was going to kill myself that night as soon as we got home. We arrived home, and he went directly into the bathroom. I went into the kitchen to get the Tylenol with Codeine and opened the bottle. I poured the pills into my hand and then down my throat (I don't know how many pills, but it was a handful). As soon as I swallowed them, his sister walked in and asked what I am doing? I told her I could not take him beating me anymore, and she called the ambulance. He did not even know what was going on because he was in the bathroom getting high. By the time the ambulance got there, he was high but still was able to give them information about me. He rode to the hospital with me and said if I didn't die, he was going to kill me. Well, I did not die, and as you can tell, he did not kill me. I was so disappointed and upset with God because I was still alive, but I stayed in the hospital for a few days, got put on medication, and was diagnosed with depression and post-traumatic stress syndrome. I asked God why He did not let me die. My kids and family would have been better off without me, but God had other plans for my life. I did not see or know them then. If He had closed my eyes for good back then, I know the life and happiness I would have missed.

There was so much physical, emotional, and mental abuse I encountered that I would need five books to explain them all. One thing I can honestly say is that I could not save myself, but I made sure that my children were saved. My children spent a lot of time with my parents and my sister. I knew they were safe, I was okay, dealing with my drama. I kept telling myself that he was going to change. He was going to be that loving man I fell in love with. My mind was so twisted that I felt I was getting everything I deserved. I felt he would finally kill me one day and put me out of my misery. After each beating, I would pray it was the last. "This time, I pray he will hit me so hard I will lose consciousness and die." My wish never came true. After each hit, I would still get up. So, I felt that was going to be how I would spend the rest of my life.

At one point, things were not all bad. After I would leave and come back, he would treat me like a queen. He would shower me with love and affection; he would basically do everything for me. Throughout our eight years together, I had a total of three miscarriages, normally after a beating would happen. I had another attempt at an unsuccessful suicide. I got so mad at myself the last time in my attempt to end my life. I said, "Damn I cannot even kill myself right." I felt I could not do anything right. There were three attempts at suicide, and I was still here. *What in the world is wrong with me?* I thought. You see, I had never known anyone besides my mother who had been abused, so I never knew that you could make it without your abuser. I should have just opened my eyes and looked at my mother. She was a survivor. She lived to live again, and she was no longer being abused. For some reason, I had the mindset that I was going to change my husband, even if it killed me, and it literally almost did.

I just did not understand myself. Why don't I just leave? That was my main question, but I did not know how to leave. There were no places I could go for help and guidance. This was in the early 90's. Domestic violence was not really taken serious then. There were no advocate groups I knew of. Even if there were, I did not know how to ask for help. Through all of this, I continued to work when I could. No one at work would ask about my various injuries or my bruises, so I felt I was not going to get any help there. I went to church every week, and I really can't say if I had bruises or not, but I am sure if I did. I had them covered up by make-up. I never made eye contact with anyone, but I know I felt peace in church but could not find peace within myself. One thing that was never taken from me was my love for God and my faith in him, but I had no faith in myself. Yes, I was a Christian, a mother, and a wife, but I was wearing a mask. As I look back, I know I was not the type of mother my children deserved. I thank God for family because they stepped in and did the things I couldn't or was not able to do.

Through all the hurt, pain, and disappointment, I still had some hope of being free one day, but I knew it had to take a miracle. I often wondered, *why am I going through this? Why won't God just let me die?*

Why does He keep saving me to live through this abuse again? Never did I realize the answer to all my questions would come later in life.

Well, I am sure most understand when there is a shift. It could either be a good or a bad shift. This shift began bad but turn out to be a good one. It was early spring or summer of 1995. I finally broke free, but not after almost losing my life behind his physical abuse. I will never forget that day. It was a Sunday. The kids and I had gone to church, and I felt different from the time I woke up until the moment I walked into the church. See, he never stopped me from serving God, but I just wish I knew how to open my mouth and tell someone what I was going through. We had already programmed the kids, "What happens in our home, stays in our home." That is what I learned as a child. I have told this part of my journey several times. Each time, it shows how much God absolutely loved me because it was by His grace and mercy that I made it out. Okay, let me slow down and tell the story. As I walked through the doors of the church, I could literally feel the Spirit of the Lord walking the aisles. I sat in my pew and cried and cried some more. I even prayed to God to be finally set free from the Hell I was living every day. I was so deep into the Spirit that I got up from my seat and took off running around the church. This was something I had never done before. I had seen it done and had even talked about people doing it, but God was doing something to me on the inside. I just could not sit still. God does hear our prayers, and He will answer your prayers in his own time. After church was over, my mother dropped us off at home, and my husband and I cooked a wonderful dinner. He played with the kids. We sat and talked, and we were having a great time as a family. He then gave the boys a bath and got them ready for bed. I just knew we were going to have a nice evening, just enjoying each other's company. Well, it did not work that way. As we sat at the dinner table, he looked me straight in my eyes and said, "God told me to kill you tonight." I did not say a word. I just looked at him. He kneeled in front of a picture we had of God on the wall. He said, "I hear you, Lord. I will do it tonight." The next thing I knew he slapped me so hard my bottom lip began to bleed. He walked me to the bathroom to get a towel and cold water to help stop the bleeding. Then, he took me into the bedroom and had me to get out of all my clothes. He beat me, but there was something different this time. I could not cry nor scream. I believe that is what made him even more angry. I only knew what he had just shared. God told him to kill me, so I believed this was going to be it. He tried to unplug the iron we had on the dresser, but for some reason, he could not move the dresser to get it unplugged. He grabbed a can of spray starch and begin to hit me over the head repeatedly. The can was new, so there were some hard blows to the head and face. Again, I still could not scream or cry. He said I was going to die that night. He left out of the room, and I could hear him in the kitchen drawer. As I stood there dripping in blood from my busted lip and head hurting. I could feel my lip swelling up. I knew what he was looking for, the big kitchen knife we had. I had already cleaned the kitchen, so the knife was in the drain board under the pots and pans. As I stood in the doorway of the bedroom in shock, I could not move, and I began to pray for my children and family. This was an unselfish prayer. I did not pray for myself. I wanted God to look out for my babies and for them to have no memory of my abuse. They were in the other room. I was not sure if they were asleep or not, but all I could pray about was them and my family. I wanted God to let them know I loved them, and none of this was their fault.

As I looked down the hall, I could still hear him looking for the knife. It really felt like an eternity, but I guess it was only a few minutes.

So much was going through my head besides the pain I was feeling. My eyes were beginning to swell, and my vision was becoming blurred. I could not take my eyes off the front door. I looked at the locks, which were deadbolted and locked. Because we lived in an apartment, we would also lock both locks when we came into the house. As I stood there with only a pair of socks on, naked, dripping in blood, with blurred eyes and a pounding headache, I continued to pray for the safety of my children. At this time, everything was beginning to seem so far away. My eyes were swelling more and more until I could barely see, but I still stood in the bedroom doorway with them focused on that front door. I was not sure if I was imagining things, or did the front door open? All I remember is running down the hallway and out the door. When I realized I was on the other side of it, I ran as if my life depended on it, and it did. I ran so hard that I ran out of my sock, so there I was running through an apartment complex looking for any light that may have been on. It was around four am in the morning. I kept running. I looked ahead and saw the light on in an apartment, and that was the door I knocked on. Remember, I was naked, bleeding, and could barely see out of my eyes. The man who answered the door immediately grabbed my arms and pulled me into his apartment. He gave me some sweatpants and a t-shirt to wear and called the police. The police arrived, took my report, took pictures, and they went to the apartment. Of course, he was gone, but the children were safe in their room crying. A few days later, I had to go before the judge to get a protective order. I had to show the judge my identification because of the pictures taken by the forensic unit of the police department that night of the injuries and the way I appeared in court. The judge said I did not look like the same person. In just a few days the swelling in my face had gone down, my lip was not swollen, and my eyes (instead of blood shot) were wide open and bright. God had done a miracle to my face, and at that moment, I did not look like what I had been through. Those pictures were so horrible, and I was so unrecognizable. Anyway, I was able to get that piece of paper that did not do anything to protect me from that monster, who would always find me. It did not matter how many times he found me. He never had that much control over me again, and he never hit me again. He was later diagnosed as bipolar, multiply personality disorder. There is so much more that I could tell you about this part of my life, but I am happy to report that in 1996 we were divorced, and I was finally set free from bondage, so I thought.

CHAPTER FOUR

A DIM LIGHT FLASHING

I am sure you are saying, "Now, I know this girl was glad to be free." Well, in a way, I was, but in a way, I was not. After so many years of abuse, it became a normal way of life for me. With me having to make a life for myself, I honestly did not know how.

Let us think back a little. From birth to eighteen years old, I lived at home. My first marriage was at the young age of nineteen, which ended in divorce. I was remarried at twenty-two and divorced at thirty. I had always lived my life with someone other than myself. Now, I had to learn how to be a single parent and raise these two boys on my own. How was I supposed to do that? How was I supposed to move forward? Guess what? I did.

It was not easy, but then I begin to find my way. I was smiling again. My boys and I were able to go outside and play, without worry if we were going to be found, or if someone was going to try and to kill us. As time went on, I began to notice some disturbing behavior out of my youngest son. He was always angry. He would get mad at a drop of a hat. Well, I should have known that would happen. All he had witnessed was violence and anger, so why would he not mirror that?

The good thing about it was that I was always able to get help for my boys and made sure they were safe but never looked out for myself. I reached out to the men at my church. They took them both under their wings and help them become young men and changed things in their lives. I will forever be grateful to the men of Oak Hill Missionary Baptist Church in Dallas, Texas.

The boys and I moved in with my mother, which was great. We were building on our relationship. Still, there is nothing like having your own place. I finally found the boys and I a wonderful place to live, and I was working full time again. They were attending school. Everything was looking up. That broken light in our life was beginning to shine again. However, it did not shine for long. I let my guard down and allowed the boys to go outside and play while I was in the house cooking dinner. As I turned to look toward the front door of the apartment, I saw my oldest walking in the house, followed by my youngest, and his father was right with him. My heart dropped, and I immediately began to worry and sweat. I wondered how he found us. I thought I was being careful. He walked into the apartment like we have been together the whole time. He walked over, kissed me, and said, "Baby I am home." He told the boys to go in the room and play and had me sit in the living room. He bragged about how he had gotten his life together and how he was ready to come home. He reached into his pocket and took out a gun. I just knew that was the end. Either he was going to shoot me and then kill himself, or he was going to kill us all. I played along with him and told him how much I had missed him and wanted him to find us (he knew I was lying). We sat there for maybe fifteen minutes, which of course seemed like an hour. Then, the phone rang. I told him I had to get it, or someone was going to think something was wrong with me. When I got my own place, my sister and I came up with a code word that I would use if something was not right. So, I picked up the phone, and it was her. She could tell something was wrong by the tone in my voice, and I immediately told her that I was not going to wear that pink dress (pink was our code word). We talked for a few more seconds, and I hung up. She called the police, and within minutes, they were at the house. However, he felt that he was above the law. He had forgotten I had an active protective order against him. When the police arrived at the apartment, he answered the door. After being questioned, the police asked for a copy of the lease. On the lease, it had who lived in the apartment. I was not as dumb as he thought I was, and neither was the police. On the lease, I had listed the children's name, along with their date of birth. My youngest son is a junior, so of course, they had the same name. Soon, another police officer showed up, and that is when they put him in handcuffs because the protective order was on file. As they were handcuffing him and patted him down, they found the gun. This part upsets me to this day; the police officers made a joke out of the gun being a BB gun and would not have hurt me. To me, I did not care if it was a BB gun or a real one. To me, it was a gun. Of course, they took him away, and I moved out the next weekend.

At this point, you are probably wondering how I got my divorce. Well, it was not as hard as some may think. A few months later, he got shot trying to steal drugs from a known drug dealer, and they had to amputate his leg. I went up to hospital and had my divorce papers with me. With the help of the administration, he signed, and they notarized the papers. I was finally divorced and free from him. I only had contact with him a few months after, as he wanted to see his child, but after a few visits with him, our son said he did not want to see his dad again, and he did not, at least not on my watch.

We never know the direction life is going to send us. I am still trying to adjust to living on my own and raising two boys. This was not easy, but I was doing it. We were happy, the kids were happy, and life was good. I was lonely but honestly afraid of dating. However, I dated a few young men were just as bad as the other. I dated a church boy, I dated a thug. Then, I got involved with another person who was on drugs. My track record was just repeating itself. How was I continually attracting these types of men? What was it about me? What was wrong with me? I could not figure out the how for a long time. Finally, I said enough was enough. I stopped. No more dating. No more men. I had to get to the bottom of what was wrong with me. I tried, but I never figured it out; things just got better for me, and I went through life wearing a mask. I was in and out of therapy, taking medication, and trying to find my way in life. I was not a little girl or a young adult. I was a grown ass woman who was having a hard time adjusting to life.

The mask not only covered my face; I wore a full body mask. I was always ashamed of my past and never wanted anyone to know what I had gone through. I really felt everything I had gone through was my fault. I believed I deserved it. I remember telling myself that many times. I thanked God for my children every day, but I did not know how to love myself, let along how to love them. I thank God for family and the village who helped me with my children. I was never shown love as a child. I was never shown love as a teenager or even as an adult. I went through just existing without a purpose, so I thought.

I never knew a simple phone call would change my whole life. You see, I have always been that girl who looked for love in all the wrong places. I was looking for validation in men. I was looking for someone to physically love me, not knowing the whole time I was loved by my children and family. I could not receive their love because I was too caught up in self, my selfishness, and my self-pity. It was all about me and what I wanted. I never realized I already had all I needed. I just had to tap into it. I knew who God was and what He was about, but I never had that personal relationship with Him because I thought everything was all about me. I played the victim role for so long I did not know how to break away from it. It's not like I got a lot of attention from it because only my family knew what I had gone through. I was embarrassed and did not have any friends to even talk to. I was isolated from family and friends. No one existed but him for many years. My children did not even exist; they were with family all the time. As I stated earlier, I had sense enough to get my children to safety, but I did not know how to save myself.

Well, God began to move in my life, or should I say I finally let God move in my life. I started truly studying the word of God to get a clear understanding about this journey called life. Yes, there were many lessons I had to learn and many things I brought on myself. My grandmother made sure that the foundation of God was set for me a long time ago, and she would talk and tell us how to tap into the love of God. She taught us how to receive him in our lives, and we did all of that. Again, I was still missing the point, so I thought I had tapped in. I was always looking for someone else to save me, to fix things for me, and to make things better. I didn't realize I had to do all of this myself, especially if I wanted a permanent fix. A temporary fix was how I lived my life for so many years. We never know where this journey called life would lead us. I never knew my journey would lead me over 1000 miles away, and it was a journey worth taking.

CHAPTER FIVE

LIVING TESTIMONY

There is a song written and sung by The Williams Brothers called, Living Testimony, the first verse sums up my whole life.

This journey called life brought me to Fayetteville, North Carolina from the big city of Dallas, Texas. This was something I never would have imagine happening in my life. I am starting my life over and was doing surprisingly well, but I was still having a hard time dealing with not being hit, slapped, or kicked. I had gone through that for so long. As I stated earlier, it was normal life for me. I do not want to say I missed it. Then again, I think I did.

Before moving to Fayetteville, North Carolina. I had gotten a full-time job at an automobile finance company, and I sometimes worked late in the evening because we did the financing for car dealerships in other states. One night, I was working late and received a fax. It was a finance application from a dealership in North Carolina. There was information missing, so I had to make that phone call I normally didn't like to make. Most of the car dealers were arrogant and acted as if I did not know what I was talking about. The gentleman on the other end of the phone was so pleasant and had a very sexy voice. I was conducting business as usual and so was he until we got to the end of the conversation. His whole conversation changed. At this time, I have not dated or even talked to anyone in a romantic way. I was really trying to work on me, so all I did was go to work, church, and home. In previous conversations with men, I would give the wrong telephone number. For some reason, this time, I gave this man the correct phone number. I did not realize I had until the next day. The following day I went to work early. Around lunch time, I always called home to check on the kids and my mom. Well, this day, my mom asked me who was the person from North Carolina calling me. I dropped the phone and said, "Damn, I gave that man my right number." So, I had to do some searching back through my phone log from the night before to find his phone number, and I did. I called him, and over a few weeks, we were making plans to see each other. I was totally mesmerized by his conversation. A few weeks later, I hopped my butt on a plane and went to North Carolina to meet him in person. Of course, my family thought I was crazy because I had not had a good track record with men. Then, with me going that far just to meet a man was something they could not understand. I have never flown before, and I was scared shitless, but I was willing to make the journey.

I flew into Raleigh/Durham Airport. We had seen pictures of each other but that was about it. I was so nervous. I begin to put myself down, talk about my weight, my hair, the clothes I was wearing, and just really made things worse for me. I really felt like I was about to pass out, but I didn't. A few seconds later, I turned around and he walked up to me and gave me a big hug. He was just as nervous as I was. He brought his best friend with him, and she hugged and greeted me as well. The next days were magical. He was such a gentleman. He showed me around town and took me to a club (I had never been to a club before). We danced (should I say, he taught me how to slow dance). He even introduced me to his parents, which I thought was a good thing. They fell in love with me just as I did with them. We slept next to each other every night for four days in a king-sized bed. He held me tight. We kissed but never had sex. Of course, I was saying to myself, *this man must be gay, or crazy not to want to have sex with me.* I was willing because how he treated me was worth giving him some loving, but I did not press the issue. I flew back to Texas and about six weeks later he flew to Dallas to meet my family and my children. We had a great time, and my family and children fell in love with him. Again, we slept in the bed next to each other in a hotel, and he did not make any moves on me. At this point, I said, "Yep, he is gay, and he is just playing me." So, before he left to head back to North Carolina, we had that conversation about not having sex, and he told me sex would come. We needed to get to know each other without sex being a distraction. I still thought something was wrong with him.

A few months later, I was packing my stuff and moving to North Carolina. I kept telling myself that I needed a change, I needed a new life. This big move must work. This was a hard decision to make, especially leaving my family and my children behind, so I could go and reestablish myself. It was a long drive, but I made it, and things were really going good for us until our feelings got deep. Now, it was easy for me to love, but it was so hard for him. He tried so many times to get me to leave and go back to Dallas, but I refused to be a failure again. So, I had to put on my big girl panties and make a life for myself, and I did just that. I got a job. When he realized I was not going anywhere, he jumped on board. I had two wonderful stepchildren and God even blessed us with grandchildren as well.

We drove back to Dallas, Texas a year later to pick up my boys. He was a great father to the boys and they had him wrapped around their fingers. Two years later, we got married. Johnnie was a good man; he was ten years older than me, and he pushed and encouraged me to find what my purpose was in life and go after it. I did just that. I began college and got my degree in social work. I got my master's in human services. Between all of this, I became an ordained minister. Life was good until his health started to fail. For the next ten years, our life was changing. We separated a few times but would get back together. It is hard for people to believe that we never argued. I had plenty of arguments with him, but he never raised his voice. He never raised his hands to me. There were times when he was pushing me away, telling me that I needed to find someone who could give me what he could not. By that time in our life, there was no romance. We had not made love in a while, and it was only getting worse. His whole attitude changed. He was becoming mean and began to push me away emotionally. I was emotionally drained. I worked full-time, cooked, cleaned, and helped him with his home dialysis treatments. I was becoming physically drained, but God had not taken His hands off us.

In December of 2016, he accepted his calling into the ministry. For the next year, he was a minister in training. His life had changed so much that people who knew him could not believe he was the same person. When you answer, "Yes," to God, He will work a miracle in your life, and He did just that. His health began to decline rapidly. On November 18, 2017, after eighteen years together, God called him home. While going through all of that with my husband, I was also caring for a dying father who was still in Texas. I was flying back and forth to Dallas to care for my dad. Well, two weeks after the passing of Johnnie, my father passed away. There I was planning another funeral.

No, one knew the hurt, the pain, and the anguish I was going through because I was known as the strong one. I had the reputation of being able to handle whatever was going on. Not to mention, my baby sister died in 2015, and I had yet to grieve for her. I again had to be the bigger person and keep everyone uplifted and encouraged. I would often say, "What about me? Who's going to look after me?" However, God still had me, and He was still looking after me. I had some good days, and I had some bad days, and I won't complain.

Who would have known the plans that God had for me? Who would have known that in my darkness hour, in my grief and despair, God was still looking out for me? God knew I did not need to be alone. He knew I needed someone to love and care for me. God also knew that I needed to love and care for someone. God had that ram in the bush, and his name was Rev. Michael Sean Richards, Sr. Who knew I would find love again? I was not looking and neither was he, but God knew we needed each other. We were united in marriage on March 25, 2019, and our new journey has begun. What a mighty God we serve? He will look beyond your faults and see your need. Now, when I say that I have learned a lot from this man. I never knew you would go to a bar and not actually drink and alcoholic beverage. I thought if you sat at the bar you had to purchase a drink. But he taught me that you get served your dinner meal quicker if you sat at the bar. I never knew that riding around town looking at different buildings, houses could be exciting. I never knew sitting and eating ice cream, talking and just people watching could be fun. I started having fun, I started enjoying life. I was a homebody unless it had something to do with church or I was at an event. But Michael taught me to enjoy life as much as possible and that you don't have to have a lot of money to do it. I remember the times that we would go up to Applebee's with $10 and we could sit there for hours, watching TV and talking. Michael and I would sometimes sit at home, and we would talk about the bible, review each other's sermon, and even preach to each other. Preaching to each other was the best because he is such an awesome spiritual teacher. Like I said earlier God knew exactly what I needed, when I needed it and gave me my soulmate, my partner in life, my jewel.

CHAPTER SIX

YOUR GRACE AND MERCY

As I write this next chapter, I would not be here without God's grace and mercy. What the devil meant for evil, God turned it around for good. For you see, there has been a target on my life since the beginning. The devil was trying to kill me, but God's Grace and Mercy brought me through. I think about how my several attempts of unsuccessful suicide did not kill me. When you realize and understand that God is the one who carried you through you hard times, whether good or bad, God's got you. None of this would have been possible without me having a personal relationship with God. I am quite sure, after reading the previous chapters, you can say I went through hell and back. Most would say I should be crazy or in some type of institution, but God. Can I say that again? But God! I often wondered, *where am I going from here? What is next in my life?* There is so much more of my life that I could tell you about. Trust and believe, I am not telling my story for pity or for someone to feel sorry for me. I made it, and there are many who did not. I am here to tell you my story, my testimony, of how God brought me over the rough side of the mountain. There is something about that name Jesus. There is power in the name of Jesus. I am here to tell someone, "If I can make it, you can too, regardless of who you are." Do not let them who said you were not going to amount to anything define who you are or are going to be. When you see them, remind them, through your works, that God is able. God is a healer. God is a provider. God is a way maker. God is who He said He is, the Alpha, the Omega, the beginning and the end.

Your beginning may have been rough. Your middle may have been even worst, but your end can be just as God ordained it to be, great. Walk into your destiny with your head held up high. Walk in confidence, through your visible and non-visible scars, through your self-inflicted scars, or at the hands of another. You can make it. Let no one control your future but God. This journey called life is not easy, and no one said it would be, but it is so fulfilling and so worth it. I thank God for the failed attempts of suicide. I cannot imagine not being around to see my children become men, husbands, and fathers, to see my grandchildren grow up and find their paths in life. My journey is not complete. I know there is more happiness, more love, and more stories to be told.

ALL EYES ON HER STILL

Now that you know my story, do you still want to be like me when you grow up? You must be careful of what you ask for. Some people may not have been able to survive the hell I went through just to get to this point in my life.

Know your purpose in life, whether it be a writing, a singer, an actor/actress, a minister, choir director, a missionary, or mentor. Whatever your purpose is, give it 100%, and give it back to God. Identify the areas of your life that are not of God and decide to make a change but know that change does not come over night. Change does not come easy. Be ready and willing to put in the work, the hard work, because the test will not be easy. God has already prepared and equipped you for the journey. Whatever is keeping you from moving forward in your journey, whether it is unforgiveness, needing to be healed from past or current pain, or deliverance from your past sins, know that God is waiting on you to surrender and give it all to Him.

Forgiveness

Now this was one of the hardest steps I had to take. Going through therapy and taking medication, I really thought this step was going to be a snap. I say that because when you do not see the person who has hurt you, you really do not think about them. The person that I needed to forgive was me. For a long time, I did not realize I went through life, of course, blaming my abusers and not realizing I needed to forgive myself. I did not need to forgive myself because of what happened. I needed to forgive myself because I honestly blamed myself for what happened because I was silent. I became silent to the fact that my dad was beating my mother. I became silent because my uncle sexually abused me. I became silent because my high school sweetheart physically and emotionally abused me. I became silent because I allowed my ex-husband to rape and beat me. I had a lot to forgive myself for. When we hold on to unforgiveness, it halts our own growth and happiness. When we hold on to the hurt, the pain, and resentment we have endured at any point in our lives, we are preventing ourselves from moving forward. We are being held in bondage from unforgiveness. We need to forgive to free ourselves and allow ourselves to grow in truth and peace. There is a relief and freedom that comes with forgiveness.

Healing

Healing from insecurities was hard. I had believed what people said about me in the past, that I was nothing, or I felt I was nothing. I embraced my insecurities and covered up my feelings with a mask. I had always felt that I was going to be nothing more than what I presently am. I felt I was not complete if I did not have a man in my life. I felt I was not complete if I was not taking care of someone. I did not focus much on my visible insecurities, such as my weight, my spotty skin tone, or even the way I talked. I was stuck in the bondage of being accepted by men. They were my root of all evil, or should I say the so-called love of a man? I wanted love. I needed to be loved but not realizing that I was already loved by the best man of all, my Lord and Savior Jesus Christ.

I had finally moved past the unforgiveness I had in my heart for myself and others who hurt me. Now, it was time to work on my healing. As God was elevating me in my ministry, this step was a must. I would ask myself repeatedly, *how can you minister to the hurt or brokenhearted when you have yet to be healed from your own broken heart?* God began to put me in situations that I just did not understand.

Back in 2009, I began to participate in a support group called Survive and Conquer. This group was amazing. It was about women who have endured sexually, physical, emotional, and financial abuse, along with those who have gone through divorce and other tragedies in life. This was a Christian based group, and the focus was complete healing through the knowledge and following of Jesus Christ. At first, I just sat there. I was too ashamed to tell my story. I was too ashamed to admit I had gone through what a lot of them had gone through. I sat and listened each month as these women told their story and how God healed them from the hurt of the past. I would sit in awe at their testimony, but I also sat in disbelief that some of these women who had lived my life and look at them now. They spoke boldly about how, through the teaching, of God they have learned to forgive, heal, and be delivered from the enemies of their past. This was amazing to me because I had never been in this type of atmosphere. I began to share my story and testimony. Through prayer and continuing support, I was able to move forward in my journey of life. Another thing that helped was me finally speaking out about my past and realizing I was not alone. My journey was also someone else's journey, and it needed to be told. I started the journey of becoming a motivational speaker and started to tell my story. I was amazed at the positive reactions I got from people and how they would tell me they had gone through the same thing. I, at that time, realized I was not alone. There were others who needed to be healed just as I needed to. So, at that moment, I knew it was time to bring out the big guns and never stop telling my story. Isaiah 53:5 (KJV) tells us, "But he was wounded for our transgressions, he was bruised for out iniquities; the chastisement of our peace was upon him; and with his stripes we are healed."

Don't get me wrong, the process takes a while. It is not overnight. It takes years. I still have issues with some insecurities: my looks, if a dress fits right, or if I need to put on a girdle, or if I need a push up bra. The one issue I still deal with is my face. Because of my acne growing up, I have black marks from picking my bumps, so I, of course, wear make-up. I make sure I have on enough concealer on to cover up. So, I first had to begin to love me for me and who God created me to be.

I DON'T LOOK LIKE WHAT
I'VE BEEN THROUGH

I have had years of heartache; I have had years of pain. I have even had years of disgrace and many years of shame. I have even been persecuted and misused, **But I do not look like what I been through.**

The devil tried to steal all my dreams and then he tried to take all my joy too. He put hopelessness in cruise control, so I'd lose control and take my own life. **See, I do not look like what I been through.**

That small voice of suicide entered my head. Yes, it came. I was molested. My innocence was taken from me. Asked what were you wearing? What did you do? NO HUGS, NO LOVE, only humiliation, and shame. **But I do not look like what I been through.**

I was told that I was fat, ugly, and nobody wants you but me. Black eyes, a fractured nose, busted lip, and bruised ribs, all in the name of love. Beaten, raped, sodomized, and I knew one day it would get worse. That voice of suicide entered my head, pills went down my throat. My stomach was pumped. I was diagnosed with post-traumatic stress syndrome and depression. **But I do not look like what I have been through.**

Today, I do not look like I was molested. I do not look like I was beaten. I do not look like I was raped, and I do not even look like I attempted suicide. But what I do look like is God's Grace. I look like

God's Mercy. I look like the sun shining after the storm with tears of joy in my eyes.

For every time I felt like giving up, for every tear that was shed, for every time I cried, "I give up," God, you heard me and wiped the tears from my eyes. You broke the chains that had me bound. God, you opened the windows of Heaven. The wind blew in Grace, then Mercy followed. That is why I can shout without a doubt that I am more than a survivor! I am more than a conqueror! I am an overcomer. I can shout I AM HEALED, DELIVERED, AND HAVE BEEN SET FREE! See there is a story behind my praise because I don't look like what I've been through.

Author Detra D. Richards

ENCOURAGING SCRIPTURES

"You intended to harm me, but God intended it all for good. He brought me to this position, so I could save the lives of many people" **Genesis 50:20 (NLT).**

"Wherefore, my beloved brethren, let every man be swift to hear, slow to speak, slow to wrath: For the wrath of man worketh not the righteousness of God" **James 1:19-20 (KJV).**

"For God hath not given us the spirit of fear; but of power, and of love, and of a sound mind" **2 Timothy 1:7 (KJV).**

"For this is how God loved the world: He gave his one and only Son, so that everyone who believes in him will not perish but have eternal life" **John 3:16 (KJV).**

"God's will is for you to be holy, so stay away from all sexual sin. Then each of you will control his own body and live in holiness and honor" **1 Thessalonians 4:3-4 (NLT).**

"And the LORD answered me, and said, Write the vision, and make *it* plain upon tables, that he may run that readeth it" **Habakkuk 2:2 (KJV).**

"God is our refuge and strength, a very present help in trouble" **Psalms 46:1 (KJV).**

"Then they cried to the LORD in their trouble, and he saved them from their distress. He sent out his word and healed them; he rescued them from the grave. Let them give thanks to the LORD for his unfailing love and his wonderful deeds for mankind" **Psalms 119:19-21 (KJV).**

"I will praise thee; for I am fearfully and wonderfully made: marvellous are thy works; and that my soul knoweth right well" **Psalms 139:14 (KJV).**

ACKNOWLEDGMENTS

Writing this book was not an easy assignment. This wasn't anything like a school essay. This was a true assignment from God. When I co-authored my first book in 2017, there were feelings that erupted in me. I never knew the pain and suffering I had endured could help someone heal from the struggles of their life.

First and foremost, I want to thank God for His protection, love, grace, and mercy over my life. God kept me through the worst of times, the times when I was at my lowest and attempted suicide, the times when I did not want to wake up. When I did not know how to love myself, God continued to show me unconditional love.

There are so many people who, over the years, have encourage me to use my voice, who have pushed me beyond my comfort zone, and allowed me to speak on many platforms. God has surrounded me with a village of loving and caring men and women of God who see His glory all over me. If I attempt to begin naming them all, I may miss one, and I don't want to leave anyone out. Those who are close to me know who you are, and I am grateful to have each of you in my corner. This process has brought out many emotions, some good and some bad, but through it all, I can still say I made it.

To my sons Andra' and Leland, you guys are my rock, my inspiration. Out of everything you all have witnessed as children growing up, you did not let your pasts destroy who you are. Thank God for protecting your minds, your bodies, and your souls from the evil you all encountered as children. Your eyes have seen things no child should have seen. Your ears heard things no child should have heard. I have said this before and I will say it again, I am so sorry for putting you through the trauma you witnessed. I am sorry for being so weak of a woman that I could not save you from what you experienced. I am proud of you both and how you took your pain and turned it into something good. Continue to keep God first in all you do. Remember, there is nothing in life you cannot survive. I love you to infinity and beyond.

To my mother, Vivian Harris, there is so much I could say. One thing for sure, YOU TOO ARE A SURVIVOR. I want to first start off by saying I am sorry for blaming you for the trauma I experienced as a child. I blamed you and dad for not protecting me from the evil that lived in our house. I blamed you and dad for not seeing what was happening to me. How could you have known when I did not open my mouth and tell what was happening to me? But out of fear, I kept silent and went through life with hatred in my heart. After the release of my first book, we spoke openly for the first time about the elements of the past. From that day forward we have been closer than any mother and daughter could be. Yes, you had your trauma of being a victim of domestic violence and you have survived to tell your story. Although not written in book form, I have seen your story with my eyes. Finally, thank you to my wonderful stepfather, Charles Harris, for always coming to my rescue, never judging me, and always being the father figure I needed in my life. I love each of you very much.

To my loving husband, Rev. Michael Sean Richards, Sr, man you never knew the baggage you were getting. You look beyond my faults, tragedies in life, my childhood and adult trauma and chose to love me. You encouraged me to do all that God has set out for me. Without hesitation, when I said I wanted to finish my book, you encouraged me to write. You offered to leave the house when I was writing so you could not distract me. When we met four years ago, we had no idea the plans God had for our lives. What a journey God has set us on, and he has ordered our steps to be great. I appreciate how you lift me up when I have a bad day. I appreciate you being in my corner when I cannot find the words to say or write. Thank you for loving me, praying for me, and being here with me. Thank you for allowing me to be me. You have the uncanny ability to have me look at things differently and not as you see them. You are eager to show me how to enjoy life and how to continue to grow in God. Michael Richards, I thank God for you daily, and I pray God will continue to allow us to grow together and build the Kingdom of God that you have birthed us to do.

To my Grace Temple Church family for always having my back, for always believing and supporting me. Whatever event I am scheduled to speak at, to every program I have sponsored y'all have always showed up and showed out. Thank you does not seem enough but you each know how I feel about you. Out of all the unordinary services we have each Sunday, we know that the best is yet to come. I love each of you to the moon and back. Not, only did God see the best in me, so do you.

ABOUT THE AUTHOR

Detra Denise Richards is a wife, mother, and grandmother who currently works as a hospital social worker. Detra is also an ordained minister, which earned her the title of an evangelist.

She is affectionately known as Evangelist Detra Denise Richards. Detra acquired her bachelor's degree in social work from Methodist University at age 47. She was inducted into the Phi Alpha Honor Society. After completion of her bachelor's degree, she further pursued a higher degree, and in 2017, she obtained a master's in human services from Capella University. Again, she was inducted as a member of Tau Upsilon Alpha-Beta Chi Honor Society. Detra's life has been about tolerance and endurance as she had to bear through the wounds of domestic violence. She believes this experience should be likened to an iron passing through furnaces, heat, and pressure to forge a sharper sword. Detra's experience with domestic violence has made a stronger woman and a more determined woman to never be silent and ashamed of her past. . She has learned how to stop hiding behind the mask of fear and caring about what people may say and think about her.

She is an associate minister at Grace Temple Church, where she has the honor of preaching the Word of the Lord to all those who attend. Detra has openly spoken about her battle with depression, low self-esteem, attempted suicides, and physical and sexual abuse. She has used this platform that God has set upon her to tell her testimony near and far. She has been challenged by herself and other victims to never keep silent and stand on the promises of God that He will never leave you or forsake you. God is forever guiding her in new directions.

Detra is also an active member of Women of Triumph Ministries International, whose mission is to strengthen women and support families and to empower them to become productive in their communities.

For those who have a similar story to hers, she hopes her story will be a source of courage and strength to face and conquer the challenges and be a proud survivor of domestic violence.

His Glory Creations Publishing, LLC is an International Christian Book Publishing Company, which helps launch the creative fiction and non-fiction works of new, aspiring and seasoned authors across the globe, through stories that are inspirational, empowering, life-changing or educational in nature, including poetry, journals, children's books, and recipe books.

DESIRE TO KNOW MORE?

Contact Information:
CEO/Founder: Felicia C. Lucas
www.hisglorycreationspublishing.com
Email: hgcpublishingllc@gmail.com
Phone: 919-679-1706

www.ingramcontent.com/pod-product-compliance
Lightning Source LLC
Chambersburg PA
CBHW051708090426
42736CB00013B/2593